aud

Di azé

Translated by Babyl Traducciones

101 Dates in French History

told to children

Éditions Jean-Paul Gisserot

www.editions-gisserot.eu

For 1,600,000 years : hominids, then men have occupied the territory.

First, these hunters improved techniques for carving stone. Then, they mastered the fire 500,000 years ago. In the Upper Paleolithic, around 35,000 BC, the first modern men, belonging to the homo sapiens sapiens species, developed artistic production and beliefs.

Around 31,000 BC : setting of the Chauvet-Pont-d'Arc cave in the Ardèche.

420 representations of animals : bears, horses, felines, bison, rhinos... and even a half-man, half-animal figure have been painted or engraved on the walls. Prehistoric Man also adorns the caves of Arcy-sur-Cure in the Yonne region around 26,000 BC and the Lascaux cave in the Dordogne region, the most famous in France, around 15,000 BC.

Towards 5000 BC : first traces of an agricultural activity.

The cultivation of cereals promotes the development of clustered habitat in the form of huts. The Neolithic Man is settling down. The ceramic technique is spreading.

4500 BC to 1500 BC : megalithic societies and the development of metallurgy.

The menhirs, isolated or aligned erected stones as in Carnac in Morbihan or in Corsica, undoubtedly have social and religious functions. Dolmens and covered alleys, sort of stone chests, are tombs. Copper craftsmanship appeared around -2800 BC, bronze around 2800 BC. The Iron Age, from 1800 BC, is particularly associated with the Celtic civilization.

Around 600 BC : founding of Massalia (Marseille) by Greeks from Phocaea.

This fortified city is a commercial port through which wine from Italy and ceramics imported from Greece, Southern Italy and Sicily transit. The Romans founded Narbonne, their first colony in Gaul, in 118 BC.

52 BC : conquest of the entire Gaul by the Romans.

Vercingetorix, son of a Gallic chief of the Arvernes tribe, was defeated at Alesia by Julius Caesar's legions. The Gallo-Roman civilization then flourished with the construction of cities such as Lyon or Autun, equipped with temples, theatres, thermal baths, and supplied with water by aqueducts such as the Pont du Gard.

177 : Saint Pothin, bishop, and Saint Blandine martyred in Lyon in the amphitheatre of the Three Gauls.

The Christian religion was persecuted by Roman authorities until the Edict of Milan in 313. The bishop leads the community from the capital city. A network of bishoprics developed from the 3rd century onwards. Saint Martin, bishop of Tours, founded the first monastery in Ligugé in 361. The countryside is slowly christianized.

End of the 5th century : establishment of the Romano-Barbarian kingdoms in Gaul.

The last Roman emperor of the West, Romulus Augustule was deposed in 476. The Franks dominate the north of Gaul, the Visigoths Aquitaine from Toulouse, the Burgundians a territory between Geneva, Dijon and Avignon, and the Ostrogoths Provence.

Around 498 (or 508?) : Clovis, king of the Franks, is baptized by Bishop Remi in Reims.

Around 498 (or 508?): Clovis, king of the Franks, is baptized by Bishop Remi in Reims. This pagan king, who supposedly descends from a chief called Merove, gained the support of the bishops and Gallo-Roman people through his conversion to Catholicism. He and his descendants formed the Merovingian dynasty which gradually dominated Gaul and reigned until 751.

732 : Battle of Poitiers.

The Arabs, who had been established in Spain since 711, carry out devastating raids on Frank territory. Charles Martel, mayor of the palace, helps the Duke of Aquitaine Eudes against them. At Moussais-la-Bataille, near Poitiers, he wins a victory that designated him as the true strong man of Frankish Gaul to the detriment of the Merovingian king

751 : Pépin le Bref, mayor of the palace, is elected king by the Franks.

Pépin sends the last Merovingian king to a monastery and takes power. It is a coup d'état. He thus founded the Carolingian dynasty, named after Charles Martel, his father. In 754, Pope Stephen II consecrates Pepin the Bref King of the Franks in the Abbey of Saint-Denis, which gives the dynasty a very strong religious legitimacy.

778 : battle of Roncesvalles.

The Basques take by surprise Charlemagne's army, the son of Pépin le Bref, in this Pyrenean pass. Duke Roland dies during the fight. His resistance inspired La Chanson de Roland, a song written in the 11th century.

25 December 800 : Charlemagne is crowned Emperor in Rome by Pope Leo III.

Thanks to the efficiency of the Frankish army, Charlemagne dominates a territory of one million square kilometres where culture thrives. In a renewed network of schools, monks, clerics and a few layman studyand copy the manuscripts. The teachings are focused on the Bible and Christian authors, but profane Greek and Roman texts are also being rediscovered.

843 : Treaty of Verdun.

After the battle of Fontenoy-en-Puisaye in 841, the sons of Louis le Pieux, Charlemagne's successor, shares the Frankish territory. Charles the Bald reigns in the west, Lothaire in central France and Louis in eastern France where Germanic languages are mainly spoken. This treaty helps to separate France and Germany.

845 : first siege of Paris by the Vikings.

These Scandinavians or "Normans" (the "northern men") sail up the rivers on their flat-bottomed boat, the snekkar, later called drakkar; they loot or collect tributes. In 911, King Charles the Simple hoped for peace by granting them a territory which became Normandy.

987 : Hugues Capet is elected King of the Franks.

Louis V, the last Carolingian king, dies without an heir. A nobleman, Hugues Capet, is elected king. The Capetians reigned first from a small estate around Paris. In feudal society, royal power is delegated and then monopolized by the nobility. By extending their domain, kings assert themselves against the nobility. The Capetian dynasty reigns until 1328.

11th-12th centuries : development of Romanesque art.

The economic boom makes it possible to rebuild cathedrals, abbey churches and cloisters by vaulting them. A sculpted display sometimes decorates the tympanums of church portals and capitals.

1095 : Pope Urban II preaches the first Crusade in Clermont, Auvergne.

The Holy Sepulchre of Jerusalem, which, according to Christian tradition, shelters Christ's tomb, is destroyed by a caliph in the early 11th century. The crusade, both a pilgrimage and a war of reconquest, is intended to reclaim the Holy Land. Eight crusades follow one another between 1095 and 1270. Only the first one is a real military success.

1152 : divorce of Louis VII and Eleanor of Aquitaine.

Louis VII separated from his wife Eleanor. She takes back her dowry, which is southwestern France, and offers it to her new husband, King Henry II of England, that same year. This case exacerbates the rivalry between both countries.

Late 11th to 15th century : the rise of the ogival or "Gothic" style and the first universities.

Masons from Picardy, then Normandy, support the vaults with stone arches, ribs, and external buttresses. Walls are built thinner. The natural light filtered by coloured stained glass floods buildings, just as Intelligence illuminates the thinking cultivated in the first universities from the 13th century onwards.

1204 : capture of the Norman fortress of Château-Gaillard by King Philippe-Auguste.

In 1066, the Duke of Normandy William conquers England, as the famous Bayeux tapestry tells us. The Anglo-Norman kingdom is founded, but King Philippe Auguste of France re-conquers Normandy, which King Henry III of England officially renounces in 1259.

1244 : capture of the Cathar castle of Montségur, in Ariège.

This episode illustrates the struggle of the Church and royal power against the Cathars, a word that means the "Pure". The latter are accused of spreading heresy, i. e. errors in religious matters, and thus dividing Christianity and the Kingdom of France.

1307 : King Philip the Fair has the Knights Templar arrested.

This order of monk soldiers founded in 1120 is responsible for protecting pilgrims to the Holy Land and becomes rich. The king, in financial difficulty, hopes to seize their property. He accuses the Knights Templar of heresy and obtains their suppression from the Pope at the Council of Vienna in 1312.

1309-1377 : the Popes in Avignon.

The election of a new Pope is an event that often causes unrest in Rome. Under the influence of King Philip the Fair, the election of the Frenchman Clement V is an opportunity for the Papacy to settle in Avignon, a quieter territory which belongs to them and where the Palais des papes is built.

1337-1453 : the Hundred Years' War between France and England.

Charles IV dies in 1328. The house of Valois then reigns from 1328 to 1589, but Edward III of England, grandson of Philip the Fair, claimed the throne of France. France is defeated in 1346 in Crecy and in 1356 in Poitiers. From 1361 to 1380, the knight Bertrand du Guesclin pushes the English back, but the latter again decimate the French nobility in Azincourt in 1415. At the Battle of Castillon in 1453, King Charles VII of France puts an end to the conflict and recovers Guyenne. The capture of Calais in 1558 completes the reconquest. At that time, the warfare adapts itself to newly imported artillery.

1347-1349 : the Black Death.

Ships hailing from a Black Sea port had taken on board rats carrying a flea which carries and transmits the plague. This disease spreads and causes the death of one-third of the population of Western Europe in a few decades. France is very affected by the epidemic.

1431 : sentencing and execution of Joan of Arc.

This young girl from Domrémy, in Lorraine, claims that celestial voices are ordering her to meet the dauphin, the future Charles VII. With a troop of soldiers, she liberates Orléans and leads the dauphin to Reims in 1429 to have him crowned king. Captured in Compiègne by the Burgundians, allied to the English, Joan of Arc is accused of heresy and burned alive in Rouen. A court ruling redeemed her in 1456.

1477 : annexation of Burgundy.

In 1363 King Jean le Bon entrusts the Duchy of Burgundy to his younger son Philippe for him and his descendants to administer. The latter then acquires territories in the North, among which Flanders. Duke Charles the Bold succeeds in unifying the whole by taking Lorraine, but is finally defeated by René II of Lorraine, financed by Louis XI, in Nancy on 5th January 1477. Ducal Burgundy is reunited with the crown of France.

1494-1559 : the Italian Wars and the Battle of Marignan in 1515.

From Charles VIII to Henry II, the kings of France have claims over the kingdom of Naples and the duchy of Milan. Eleven wars follow one another. In 1515, Francis I wins the Battle of Marignan, which gives him control over Lombardy. In 1559, with the second Cateau-Cambresis treaty, France abandons its claims on Italy.

First half of the 16th century : construction of the Loire castles.

The kings of France and prominent figures build sumptuous residences in the Loire Valley such as Azay-le-Rideau, Blois, Chenonceau, Chambord and Cheverny, where the artistic Renaissance originating from Italy blooms.

1532 : Brittany returns to the Crown.

At the request of the States of Brittany, this duchy is definitively united to France by the Edict of Plessis-Macé. The event had been prepared by the marriages of Duchess Anne of Brittany with Charles VIII in 1491 and Louis XII in 1499.

1534-1536 : Jacques Cartier in Canada.

This Saint-Malo sailor explores the Gulf of St. Lawrence and sails up the river. Contacts are established with Amerindian tribes. However, the colonization of New France, future Canada, only really begins in 1608 with the founding of Quebec City by Samuel de Champlain.

1539 : Villers-Cotterêts Order.

By this law, the king orders priests to keep a register of baptisms. The use of French instead of Latin in official documents is also required.

Night of 23th to 24th August 1572 : Saint-Barthélemy massacre.

In France, eight religious wars oppose Catholics and Protestants between 1562 and 1598. On 22nd August 1572, an assassination attempt against Admiral de Coligny triggers the anger of Protestants, of whom he is one of the leaders. To restore calm, King Charles IX orders the execution of Protestant leaders, to which popular fury triggers massacres in Paris and in the provinces.

13th April 1598 : Edict of Nantes.

Henry III recognizes his Protestant cousin Henri de Bourbon, King of Navarre as his heir. At the death of Henry III, murdered by fanatical monk Jacques Clément in 1589, Henry IV meets with opposition from Catholics. Converted to Catholicism in 1593, the first Bourbon king puts an end to the Wars of Religion with this edict of tolerance. Protestants can practice their religion and keep 51 safe places, including La Rochelle.

1610 : assassination of King Henry IV by Ravaillac.

Some Catholics have not forgiven the king for his edict of tolerance, even though it has brought peace to the kingdom. On 14th May, 1610, a mad Catholic, François Ravaillac, takes advantage of a traffic jam in Paris to murder Henri IV by stabbing him several times in his carriage, in front of the the "Crowned Heart" inn.

1628 : capture of La Rochelle.

Protestant Lords fear the restriction of their freedoms. They rebel in the hope that the English would support them. This danger leads Louis XIII and his minister, Cardinal de Richelieu, to take La Rochelle, which is an important port on the Atlantic coast.

1635 : Richelieu founded the Académie française.

One of the objectives of this institution is to set the standards for French language. It publishes the first edition of its *Dictionary* in 1694.

1642 : death of Richelieu.

Cardinal Mazarin, of Italian origin, replaces Richelieu as principal Minister of State next to Louis XIII.

1648 : by the Treaty of Westphalia, France acquires part of Alsace.

This treaty ends the Thirty Years' War which had divided Europe since 1618. Ferdinand III of Habsburg, emperor of the Holy Roman Empire, cedes a part of Alsace to France, which had coveted it since the 14th century.

1648-1653 :The "Fronde".

When Louis XIII dies in 1643, Louis XIV is only five years old. In 1648, during the regency of Anne of Austria, the Parliament rebels against the tax burden due to the war against Spain. In 1650, the nobility in turn rises against Louis XIV, but Mazarin's skills save the authority of the young king.

1661 : beginning of Louis XIV's personal reign and arrest of Nicolas Fouquet.

When Mazarin dies in 1661, the king decides not to replace him. He appoints his ministers and surrounds himself with a government composed of several specialized councils. He also imprisons superintendent of finances Nicolas Fouquet, accused of embezzlement and whose beautiful castle of Vaux-le-Vicomte seems to defy the king himself by its splendour.

From the 1660s : Louis XIV practices the economic theory of mercantilism.

The king, assisted by Colbert, controller general of finances, promotes industry and trade by creating the Commercial and Colonial Companies of India and factories. The Royal Mirror Glass Manufactory, founded in 1665, produces the mirrors for the Hall of Mirrors in Versailles. It later becomes the Saint-Gobain company.

1672 : Beginning of the Dutch War.

Decades of conflict with Spain, Holland or the Empire warrant an "iron belt" of strongholds built according to a star-shaped design by Vauban, a military engineer. Speaking of a « pré carré » (territory) Vauban urges the king to straighten the country's northern border. By annexing Strasbourg in 1681, for example.

1682 : Versailles becomes the main residence of the royal family and of the court. Architects Louis Le Vau and Jules Hardouin-Mansart, painter and decorator Charles le Brun and gardener André Le Nôtre build a magnificent palace in Versailles in place of the one Louis XIII had built from a hunting lodge. The king sets up his court there and attracts the nobility, to whom he grants pensions. As with sunlight, all authority and power comes from the king, "lieutenant of God on Earth" and "Sun King". It is the absolute monarchy of divine right.

1685 : revocation of the Edict of Nantes.

Louis XIV would like Catholicism to be the only religion in the kingdom. He revokes the Edict of Nantes. Unfortunately for the country, a Protestant bourgeoisie active in commerce chooses to emigrate. Other Protestants, the Camisards, rebel in the Cévennes in 1702. In the 18th century, Jews were victims of discrimination. In 1787, the Edict of Tolerance signed by Louis XVI recognized non-Catholics' freedom of worship.

1715 : Louis XIV dies at the age of 77, after 72 years of reign.

The devastation of the "Great Winter" of 1709, the deficit of the State, the war, epidemics and mortality within the royal family darken the end of Louis XIV's reign. At the king's death, his successor and great-grandson Louis XV is only five years old. The regency is held by Philippe, Duke of Orléans, until 1723.

1748 : philosopher Montesquieu publishes *The Spirit of Laws.*

The author demonstrates that the three powers, the executive governing, the legislative drafting laws and the judiciary exercising justice, must not be brought together in the hands of the same authority, but must be separated. He therefore criticizes this royal absolutism that Louis XV defines as follows in 1766: "it is in my person alone that sovereign power resides...".

1751-1772 : publication of the *Encyclopedia.*

It is the first French encyclopedia and an ambitious undertaking: 17 volumes of texts and 11 volumes of plates. This collective work is directed by philosopher Denis Diderot and mathematician Jean d'Alembert. The work diffuses the ideas of the Enlightenment, which are favourable to the development of science and individual freedom. It criticizes absolute monarchy.

1756-1763 : Seven Years War between France and England.

France is defeated. In 1763, under the Treaty of Paris, it has to cede to England New France, i.e. Canada and a vast territory west of the Appalachians.

1762 : Voltaire and the Jean Calas case.

The Protestant Jean Calas is executed in 1762 after being wrongly accused of killing his own son to prevent him from converting to Catholicism.
François-Marie Arouet, known as Voltaire, claims his innocence, defends the idea of religious tolerance and criticizes the Church. This triggers the hostility of the regime towards him.

1766 : acquisition of the Duchies of Lorraine and Bar-le-Duc.

After negotiations with Austria, these territories return to France upon the death of Polish king Stanislas Leszczynski, to whom they belonged and for which Louis XV had married his daughter Mary.

1768 : Corsica becomes French.

The island is sold to France by the Republic of Genoa. The army of Louis XV takes possession of it the following year.

1774 : death of Louis XV. His grandson Louis XVI succeeds him.

Louis XVI married the Austrian Archduchess Marie-Antoinette. With a solid intellectual background, he is passionate about science, speaks several languages and relaxes while hunting and locksmithing. Very scrupulous, he is hesitant about the policy to be applied. The State is heavily in debt and the King has to deal with a Parliament and a nobility opposed to the principle of an egalitarian tax that would trim their way of life.

1777 : the Marquis de La Fayette helps American insurgents against the British.

La Fayette convinces Louis XVI to participate in the American War of Independence, which leads to the victory of Yorktown in 1781. This commitment is very expensive for the kingdom. Moreover, France does not become the Americans' preferred trading partner, as the King had hoped.

24th January, 1789 : regulations for the convening of the Estates General.

Since 1302, in the event of a crisis, the king sometimes brings together representatives of the three orders which make up society: the nobility (2% of the population), the clergy (1%) and the third state (97%). Faced with a catastrophic financial situation, Louis XVI convenes the meeting for May 5, 1789 in Versailles. To do this, the three orders must elect their representatives and express their demands in grievance books.

17th June, 1789 : the representaives of the third state proclaim themselves a "National Assembly".

Faced with the manoeuvres of the nobility and the clergy to preserve their privileges, the representatives of the third state swear on 20th June not to separate until they have given a constitution to France. Sovereignty will now reside in the nation which chooses its representatives to exercise it. It is a political revolution.

14th July, 1789 : storming of the Bastille by the people of Paris.

The people of Paris seize this state prison, which is a symbol of royal arbitrariness, since the king could send someone there without judging by signing a "lettre de cachet".

Night of 4th to 5th August, 1789 : abolition of privileges.

After 14th July, peasants plunder castles and destroy registers of seigneurial rights during a movement called the "Great Fear". The representatives understand this anger and put an end to the feudal regime by abolishing the privileges of clergymen and nobles, but also those of cities, trade guilds and provinces.

26th August, 1789 : Declaration of the Rights of Man and the Citizen.

With this declaration in 17 articles, the deputies express the values of the new regime, which is certainly still monarchical, but constitutional. These "Principles of 1789" establish a legal revolution. The French are no longer the king's subjects, but citizens.

14th July, 1790 : Federation Day.

83 departments had just been created to replace the old constituencies. Their deputies gather around the king at Champ-de-Mars on the anniversary of the storming of the Bastille. It is this Federation holiday, a symbol of unity, which is commemorated by the national holiday of 14th July, instituted in 1880.

20th June,1791 : Louis XVI, on the run, is arrested in Varennes-en-Argonne.

In disagreement with revolutionary politics, the king decides to mobilize counter-revolutionary troops. His escape is interpreted as a betrayal. He loses the confidence of the representatives, despite his oath to the constitution. The monarchy is suspended on 10th August, 1792. Louis XVI was imprisoned in the Temple, then guillotined on 21st January, 1793. Marie-Antoinette suffers the same fate on 21st October.

22nd September 1792 : proclamation of the First Republic

The armies of the Revolution were victorious over the Prussians at Valmy on 20th September, 1792. The Convention, as the new parliament is named, proclaims the Republic two days later.

September 1793-July 1794 : the Convention establishes Terror.

The Republic is threatened by the external enemy and the internal Counter-Revolution. At the Convention, the Montagnards deputies, led by Robespierre, suspend freedoms and the constitution. They execute thousands of "suspects", ravage the insurgent Vendée and practice a policy of de-Christianisation described as "defanatisation". The Terror ends with the execution of Robespierre himself in July 1794.

17th November, 1796 : Bonaparte's victory at the Arcole Bridge in Italy.

This ambitious general of the Revolution, of Corsican origin, demonstrates his bravery and military skills against the Austrians.

1798 : Bonaparte's expedition to Egypt.

Sent to lead an expeditionary force to oppose the English, he wins the battle of the Pyramids against the Mamluks in Cairo. Despite the destruction of the French fleet in Aboukir's harbour by English Admiral Nelson in August, the announcement of Bonaparte's victories by bulletins reveals him as a hero.

1802 : creation of lycées (public high schools).

This institution provides general education for boys only. Its purpose is to train a republican elite. Some students can then continue their studies in the Grandes Écoles such as Polytechnique, École normale supérieure or Conservatoire national des arts et métiers, founded under the Revolution.

2nd December, 1804 : Napoleon's imperial coronation.

First consul in November 1799, consul for life in 1802, Bonaparte crowns himself Emperor in Notre-Dame cathedral in Paris in the presence of Pope Pius VII. This same year, Napoleon orders the publication of the Civil Code, which regulates life in society. The Empire is a very authoritarian regime restrictive of individual freedoms.

1805-1810 : Napoleon's victories at the head of the Grand Army.

Military successes follow each other,.Notably in 1805 in Austerlitz against the Austrians and Russians, although England inflicted Trafalgar's naval defeat on France the same year. In 1812, Napoleon attacked Russia, but the terrible Russian winter forces him to retreat. The crossing of the Berezina River in November is catastrophic. Napoleon loses 500,000 men during this campaign.

1814-1815 : the Hundred Days and the defeat of Waterloo.

After the defeat of Leipzig in 1813, the war is fought in France. The emperor is defeated and abdicates on 6th April, 1814. Louis XVIII, brother of Louis XVI, reigns during the first Restoration. Exiled on the island of Elba, Napoleon escapes and returnes to reign for a hundred days. Beaten in Waterloo on 18th June, 1815, he definitively abdicates on 22nd June. Deported to the English island of St Helena, far in the South Atlantic, he dies there in 1821.

1815 : The second Restoration establishes the return of the Bourbons to the throne of France.

The second Restoration establishes the return of the Bourbons to the throne of France. The return to fundamental freedoms is guaranteed by the Charter granted in 1814 by Louis XVIII. The monarchy is constitutional, but the electoral system is restricted by the so-called "censitaire" suffrage system, because it is conditioned by taxation. In the Chamber of Deputies, the debates are between ultra-Royalists and Liberals. Louis XVIII reigns until 1824, and his brother Charles X until 1830.

1822 : invention of photography by Joseph Nicéphore Niépce.

Experiments carried out by Niépce in Chalon-sur-Saône are continued in the 1830's by Louis Daguerre.

1830 : France's conquest of Algeria.

Taking advantage of the weakness of the government of Algiers under the control of the Turks, the French army takes this city in 1830. However, the conquest of the territory is only effective after the surrender of Emir Abd-el-Kader in 1847. Algeria becomes a French colony.

27th, 28th and 29th July, 1830 : The "Three Glorious Days".

Charles X favours ultra-Royalists and Catholicism. Authoritarian, he dissolves the Chamber of Deputies and suspends press freedom. The people of Paris revolts and forces him into exile. Duke Louis-Philippe d'Orléans becomes king of the French. The July monarchy, which is constitutional, is more liberal than the previous one: it adopts the tricolour flag and Catholicism is no longer a state religion. The Guizot laws introduce public primary education in 1833.

February 1848 : proclamation of the Second Republic.

The already large working class faces very difficult working conditions and an economic crisis erupts in 1847. In rebellion, the people of Paris drive Louis-Philippe away. The Second Republic is proclaimed and, in December 1848, Prince Louis-Napoleon Bonaparte, Napoleon I's nephew, is elected president by universal male suffrage in the same year.

27th april 1848 : abolition of slavery.

Under the influence of the Alsatian deputy Victor Schoelcher, the decree on the abolition of slavery in the colonies is adopted by the Republic.

1852 : the Second Empire.

On 2nd December, 1851, Louis-Napoléon Bonaparte organizes a coup d'état after which he claims all the powers. In 1852, he has the restoration of the Empire approved by referendum. He is proclaimed Emperor on 2nd December. In 1860, Nice and Savoy become French with the Treaty of Turin. The country's industrialization is progressing.

4th September 1870 : proclamation of the Third Republic.

The war with Prussia leads to Napoleon III's defeat at Sedan on 2nd September, 1870. The Third Republic is proclaimed at the Hôtel de Ville in Paris by Léon Gambetta. A new National Assembly is elected and is based in Bordeaux. It elects Adolphe Thiers as the head of state and chief of a government which moves to Versailles. France loses Alsace and Moselle, which become German by the Treaty of Frankfurt on 10th May, 1871.

1871 : the Paris Commune

In Paris, the French capitulation causes humiliation and a fear of a return to monarchy. An insurrectional Parisian government with a socialist tendency, the Commune, is formed. Then, the soldiers of Adolphe Thier'government, the "Versaillais", besieges the capital. They put an end to the Commune at the cost of several thousand deaths among the Communards during "Bloody Week", from 22nd to 29th May, 1871.

1881-1882 : Jules Ferry school laws.

Primary education is now secular and free, but compulsory up to age 13. For the men of the Third Republic, it is a question of training republican political consciences in order to strengthen the regime and the unity of the country.

1885 : biologist and chemist Louis Pasteur develops the vaccine against rabies.

This scientist, who also invented pasteurization and recommended asepsis in hospitals, is at the origin of the Institut Pasteur, inaugurated in 1888 by President of the Republic Marie François Sadi Carnot.

1887-1889 : construction of the Eiffel Tower.

The Industrial Revolution favoured the metallurgical production of iron and steel, as evidenced by the construction of this iron tower by Gustave Eiffel and his collaborators for the 1889 Universal Exhibition. From an original height of 312 metres, the tower now stands at 324 metres since the installation of a DTT transmitter in 2011.

1894 : the Dreyfus affair divides the French.

Captain Alfred Dreyfus, a Jew, is wrongly accused of high treason by the general staff. Dreyfusards and antidreyfusards disagree on his guilt. Defended in particular by writer Émile Zola and pardoned in 1899 by President Émile Loubet, Dreyfus is reinstated in 1906. This case reveals the strong anti-Semitism which prevails in the country in the late 19th century. It also disrupts French political life.

1895 : invention of the cinematograph.

Brothers Louis and Auguste Lumière develop a camera and projection system which leads to the origin of the seventh art.

9th December, 1905 : Separation of Church and State Law.

Secularism appears to the government as the best way to fully guarantee individual freedom of thought and belief. The State does not recognize any religion and does not pay any clergy, except, after 1918, in Alsace and Moselle which were German at the time the law was adopted.

1909 : Louis Blériot achieves the first flight across the English Channel.

After the development of railway lines in France in 1839, aviation is the ultimate innovation in means of transportation before space technologies in the 1960's.

1914-1918 : First World War.

This conflict causes the death of one and a half million French people and considerable damage in the North of the country. Assaults during major battles such as the Marne in 1914, Verdun in 1916 or Chemin des Dames in 1917 result in bloodshed. After the armistice signed on 11th November, 1918, France recovers Alsace and Moselle

1920 : construction of the Great Mosque of Paris, inaugurated in 1926.

This complex is built to honour of the Muslims who died for France in WWI, even if Islam is not very present in the country in the early 20th century. Since 1945 and especially after decolonization, religious diversity has been strengthened in France.

1936 : the Popular Front.

This government unites a left-wing coalition under the leadership of Léon Blum. It passes laws implementing 15 days of paid holidays and a 40-hour work week. It is also the first government to have women among its members.

1940 : Vichy government and General de Gaulle's appeal.

The Second World War breaks out in 1939. France is defeated by the Germans in May 1940. Marshal Pétain signs the armistice and installs the very authoritarian government of the French State, which collaborated with Nazi Germany, in Vichy. Meanwhile, General de Gaulle takes refuge in London, from where he calls on France to resist on 18th June on the radio.

1944 : the Allies landings and the formation of a provisional government.

American and British Allies land in Normandy on 6th June and in Provence on 15th August. They reclaim the country. Paris is liberated on 25th August. From Algiers, the socially inspired provisional government of the French Republic proposes the right to vote for women and social security.

1947-1954 : the Indochina War.

French colonial territories cover 12 million square kilometres, mainly in Africa and Southeast Asia. Invoking the right of peoples to self-determination, Indochinese communists wage a war of decolonization. On 7th May, 1954, they defeat the French at Dien Bien Phu. On 21st July, the Geneva Accords recognize Vietnam's independence.

1947-1958 : the Fourth Republic.

The 1946 constitution provides that the government's action must be approved by a majority of deputies, otherwise the government is disavowed, which leads to its resignation. This ministerial instability has led to the formation of 24 governments in 12 years, while the country has to face the challenges of reconstruction and decolonization.

1954-1962 : the Algerian War.

The conflict begins on 1st November, 1954 and is presented by France as a peacekeeping operation. In fact, it is a decolonization war which claims 250,000 victims among Algerians and 30,000 on the French side. By the Evian Agreements, on 18th March 1962, Algeria becomes independent.

1957 : establishment of the European Economic Community (EEC) by the Treaty of Rome.

France is one of the 6 founding countries of this association of states along with the Federal Republic of Germany, Italy, Belgium, the Netherlands and Luxembourg. In particular, the EEC is created at the initiative of Jean Monnet to promote economic prosperity and to create the best conditions for peace in Europe.

1958-1969 : General de Gaulle and the Fifth Republic.

The Algerian crisis favours the return to power of General de Gaulle, who proposes a new constitution. The latter, approved by referendum, establishes a stable semi-presidential regime. In 1960, de Gaulle gives France nuclear weapons and, in 1962, he introduces by referendum universal suffrage for the presidential election. He has to deal with the student crisis and workers' strikes in May 1968. After an electoral failure in a referendum on regionalisation in 1969, he resigns and dies in 1970.

1969-1981 : presidencies of Georges Pompidou (1969-1974) and Valéry Giscard d'Estaing (1974-1981).

The oil crises of 1973 and 1979 put an end to the years of prosperity known as the "Glorious Thirty". However, profound social and economic changes are taking place in France. In education, comprehensive schools are established in 1975. In Paris, the Centre Georges Pompidou, inaugurated in 1977, symbolizes architectural and urban modernization, while the European Space Agency launches the first Ariane rocket in 1979 from its base in Kourou, French Guyana.

1981-1995 : François Mitterrand's presidential terms.

The left reforms society and the economy: abolition of the death penalty, freedom of the airwaves, nationalisation of large companies... However, it is confronted with rising unemployment. The Louvre Pyramid, the Opéra Bastille, the Bibliothèque nationale de France and the Arche de la Défense are the president's major projects. François Mitterrand is also pursuing European integration by signing the Maastricht Treaty in 1992, replacing the EEC with the European Union.

1995-2007 : seven-year term, then five year term of Jacques Chirac.

After dissolving the National Assembly in 1997, the right-wing president has to govern with a left-wing prime minister, Lionel Jospin, until 2002. In 2000, Jacques Chirac obtains by referendum the reduction of the presidential term from 7 to 5 years. The law on gender equality in politics is passed the same year. Internationally, he sends troops to Afghanistan in 2001, but refuses to commit the country to war in Iraq alongside the United States in 2003. On the cultural level, Jacques Chirac inaugurates in Paris the Musée des Arts premiers, quai Branly, in 2006.

2007-2017 : 5 year presidential terms of Nicolas Sarkozy and François Hollande.

In 2007, the president signs the Lisbon Treaty which strengthens the political union of Europe and François Fillon's government reforms the pensions system. The economic situation worsens due to the financial crisis of 2008 which starts in the United States and due to the increase of the public debt that followed.

2017 : Emmanuel Macron wins the presidential election.

François Hollande's former Minister of Economy and Finances wins the presidential races with his En Marche political movement. The new president wishes to overcome the traditionnal opposition between right and left. He wishes to mobilizes all abilities and energies to redress the country's economy and strenghthen its unity.

Imprimé et façonné par Pollina Luçon 85 n° d'impression : 88430
Printed in France